ISBN 978-1-332-85076-1
PIBN 10217168

This book is a reproduction of an important historical work. Forgotten Books uses state-of-the-art technology to digitally reconstruct the work, preserving the original format whilst repairing imperfections present in the aged copy. In rare cases, an imperfection in the original, such as a blemish or missing page, may be replicated in our edition. We do, however, repair the vast majority of imperfections successfully; any imperfections that remain are intentionally left to preserve the state of such historical works.

1 MONTH OF
FREE
READING

at

www.ForgottenBooks.com

By purchasing this book you are eligible for one month membership to ForgottenBooks.com, giving you unlimited access to our entire collection of over 1,000,000 titles via our web site and mobile apps.

To claim your free month visit:

www.forgottenbooks.com/free217168

Normandy American Cemetery

and Memorial

The American Battle Monuments Commission

The Spirit of American Youth.

2

Normandy American Cemetery and Memorial

LOCATION

Normandy Cemetery is situated on a cliff overlooking the English Channel, northeast of St. Laurent-sur-Mer, 10 miles west of Bayeux, Calvados. Nearby also, to the south, is the village of Colleville-sur-Mer. The main highway (N–13) from Paris to Cherbourg passes 3 miles south of the cemetery which is 272 kilometers (170 miles) from Paris, and is reached by leaving this highway either at Bayeux over D–6 to Port-en-Bessin thence over N–814, or at Formigny, taking N–814e.

To reach the cemetery by railroad, there is an infrequent service between Paris (Gare St. Lazare) and Bayeux, where taxicab service is available. Travel by rail takes from 4 to 6 hours each way. Hotel accommodations are available at Caen and Bayeux; there are also some smaller hotels at Port-en-Bessin (7 miles from the cemetery) and at other nearby shore resorts.

The cemetery may also be reached by automobile from Le Havre in about four hours. The Seine is crossed by several ferries whose schedule is subjcet to tide conditions; it takes little longer to go via the bridge at Rouen.

View of Portion of Graves Area—English Channel in Background.

3

Aerial View of Cemetery and Omaha Beach.

Location of Cemetery Features.

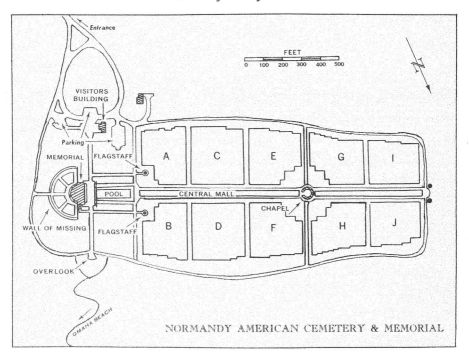

THE SITE

The cemetery site covers 172.3 acres and overlooks Omaha Beach. Here, on 6 June 1944, after crossing the Channel from England, the U. S. 1st and 29th Divisions landed on this heavily fortified shore. The site of the cemetery lay in the sector of the 1st Division. At the cost of heavy casualties, American troops seized this high ground the first day and thus established an initial foothold on the continent.

Thirty-three road miles to the west is Utah Beach where on that same morning American troops made another amphibious assault as well as an airborne landing. To the east of the cemetery are the beaches over which troops of the British Commonwealth landed.

In Normandy American Cemetery rest 9,386 of our Dead, representing 39 percent of those who were originally buried in temporary cemeteries in the region extending westward from Omaha Beach to Utah Beach and to Cherbourg, and for some miles to the south. Most of these Dead gave their lives in the landing operations and in the establishment of the beachhead.

Use of the site granted in perpetuity by the French government includes a right-of-way, ½-mile long, leading from highway N–814 to the cemetery entrance.

ARCHITECTS

Architects for the cemetery and memorial were Harbeson, Hough, Livingston & Larson of Philadelphia, Pa. The landscape architect was Markley Stevenson, also of Philadelphia.

GENERAL LAYOUT

The approach road starts at the large stone directional arrow on highway N–814 and runs between characteristic Normandy hedgerows to the main gate in the southeast corner of the cemetery. To the west of the gate is the utilities area; in this area are the deep wells which supply the cemetery water; here, too, are the reservoirs and pumping station. The Visitors' Building is situated a few hundred yards beyond the main gate. Beyond the Visitors' Building are the graves area, the memorial, the chapel, and the sea.

The Memorial

The memorial consists of a semicircular colonnade with a loggia at each end. On the platform immediately west of the colonnade is a 22-foot bronze statue "The Spirit of American Youth" rising from the waves, a tribute to those who gave their lives in these operations. Around its base is the inscription "MINE EYES HAVE SEEN THE GLORY OF THE COMING OF THE LORD". The sculptor was Donald De Lue of New York City; the bronze was cast in Milan by the Battaglia Foundry.

The frieze of the colonnade bears this inscription:

"THIS EMBATTLED SHORE, PORTAL OF LIBERATION, IS FOREVER HALLOWED BY THE IDEALS, THE VALOR AND THE SACRIFICES OF OUR FELLOW COUNTRYMEN."

On the walls within the SOUTH LOGGIA are three maps engraved in the stone and embellished with colored enamels. The largest, oriented with south at the top, portrays the landings on 6 June 1944, the establishment of the firm beachhead, the liberation of Cherbourg and St. Lô, and the subsequent attack by which our forces broke out of the beachhead.

The map on the west wall vividly depicts the air operations prior to the landings, including the isolation of the beachhead area by the destruction of all routes of access from the interior

The Memorial—West Facade.

of France; the map also records the major air operations in the beachhead after the landings.

The map on the east wall shows the Naval plan for the landings and the manner in which it was executed.

The following text, inscribed on the west wall, amplifies the maps (a French version is inscribed on the east wall):

THE ASSAULT AND THE BEACHHEAD

MANY MONTHS OF PLANNING AND DETAILED PREPARATION PRECEDED THE ALLIED LANDINGS IN NORMANDY. THE AIR BOMBARDMENT TO ISOLATE THE BATTLEFIELD BEGAN IN MARCH 1944. DURING THE NEXT THREE MONTHS THE ALLIED AIR FORCES, BY SYSTEMATICALLY BOMBING BRIDGES AND RAIL CENTERS, DISRUPTED ALL FORMS OF TRANSPORTATION BETWEEN THE SEINE AND THE LOIRE; MEANWHILE STRATEGIC AIR OPERATIONS WERE CONTINUED DEEP INTO ENEMY TERRITORY TO COMPEL THE GERMAN AIR FORCE TO REMAIN ON THE DEFENSIVE.

IN THE DARKNESS OF THE EARLY MORNING HOURS OF 6 JUNE THREE AIRBORNE DIVISIONS (THE BRITISH 6, THE U. S. 82D AND 101ST) DROPPED BEYOND THE BEACHES TO DESTROY ENEMY FORCES AND TO COVER THE DEPLOYMENT OF THE SEABORNE ASSAULT TROOPS. SIMULTANEOUSLY THE ALLIED NAVAL FORCES SWEPT THE ENGLISH CHANNEL OF MINES AND PRECEDED THE ASSAULT VESSELS TO THE LANDING AREAS. AT 0630 HOURS, UNDER COVER OF NAVAL GUNFIRE AND AIR BOMBARDMENT, SIX U. S., BRITISH AND CANADIAN DIVISIONS LANDED IN THE GREATEST AMPHIBIOUS ASSAULT RECORDED IN HISTORY.

AT UTAH BEACH, THE U. S. 4TH DIVISION PUSHED RAPIDLY INLAND TO JOIN THE U. S. AIRBORNE DIVISIONS. AT OMAHA BEACH, PROGRESS OF THE U. S. 1ST AND 29TH DIVISIONS WAS SLOWER, CASUALTIES WERE HEAVIER, THE FIGHTING BITTER. ON GOLD, JUNO AND SWORD BEACHES, THE BRITISH AND CANADIANS FORGED STEADILY AHEAD. WITHIN A WEEK, UNDER COVER OF CONTINUOUS NAVAL GUNFIRE AND AIR SUPPORT, THE INDIVIDUAL BEACHHEADS HAD BEEN LINKED TOGETHER.

MEANWHILE, NAVAL PERSONNEL WERE ESTABLISHING TEMPORARY ANCHORAGES AND ARTIFICIAL HARBORS BY SINKING

SHIPS AND PRE-FABRICATED CONCRETE CAISSONS. THESE EXPEDIENTS WERE OF PRICELESS AID IN THE UNLOADING OF TROOPS AND CARGO OVER THE UNSHELTERED BEACHES.

THE ALLIED ARMIES GREW RAPIDLY IN STRENGTH. DRIVING NORTHWARD, AMERICAN FORCES, AIDED BY STRONG NAVAL AND AIR BOMBARDMENT, FREED CHERBOURG ON 26 JUNE. ON 9 JULY, THE BRITISH AND CANADIANS FOUGHT THEIR WAY INTO CAEN; NINE DAYS LATER U. S. UNITS TOOK ST. LO. THE ALLIES COULD NOW UNLEASH THEIR PLANNED ATTACK TO BREAK OUT OF THE BEACHHEAD. WHILE BRITISH FORCES HEAVILY ENGAGED THE ENEMY ON THE ALLIED LEFT FLANK, AMERICAN TROOPS WEST OF ST. LO UNDERTOOK THE MAJOR EFFORT TO DRIVE THROUGH THE ENEMY DEFENSES. ON 25 JULY, FOLLOWING A PARALYZING BOMBARDMENT BY THE U. S. EIGHTH AND NINTH AIR FORCES AND THE ROYAL AIR FORCE, THE U. S. 4TH, 9TH, AND 30TH DIVISIONS OPENED A GAP IN THE ENEMY LINE WHICH WAS PROMPTLY EXPLOITED BY THE 1ST INFANTRY AND 2D AND 3D ARMORED DIVISIONS. OTHER AMERICAN FORCES PROGRESSIVELY ADDED THEIR EFFORTS, LIBERATING COUTANCES ON 28 JULY. IN A WEEK THE DRIVE HAD CLEARED AVRANCHES.

AFTER NEARLY TWO MONTHS' CONFINEMENT TO THE BEACHHEAD AREA, THE ALLIED ARMIES HAD FINALLY BROKEN INTO THE OPEN AND WERE MOVING FORWARD ON A BROAD FRONT.

The NORTH LOGGIA of the memorial contains a map executed in a technique similar to that of the south loggia maps; it records the progress of the military operations in northwest Europe from the landings in Normandy to the end of the war. Here also are descriptive texts in English and French, and the six key maps. The English text is as follows:

FROM NORMANDY TO THE ELBE

REACTING TO THE BREAK-OUT BY THE ALLIED FORCES FROM THE NORMANDY BEACHHEAD, THE ENEMY LAUNCHED A COUNTERATTACK TOWARD AVRANCHES WITH THE DESPERATE HOPE OF CUTTING OFF OUR ADVANCING COLUMNS, BUT WAS REPULSED WITH HEAVY LOSSES. THEREUPON, AMERICAN FORCES SWUNG NORTHWARD TOWARD ARGENTAN WHILE AT THE SAME TIME THE BRITISH AND CANADIANS ADVANCED SOUTHWARD ON FALAISE. THREATENED WITH ENCIRCLEMENT, THE ENEMY TURNED BACK. HARASSED BY AIRCRAFT, HAMMERED INCESSANTLY BY ARTILLERY, HIS RETREAT BECAME A ROUT. BY 22 AUGUST, THE POCKET WAS ELIMINATED.

PRECEDED BY AIRCRAFT OF THE U. S. EIGHTH AND NINTH AIR FORCES AND THE BRITISH SECOND TACTICAL AIR FORCE, WHOSE CONSTANT ATTACKS HASTENED THE DISORGANIZATION OF THE RETREATING ENEMY, THE ALLIED ARMIES CROSSED THE SEINE, LIBERATED PARIS, AND SWEPT ONWARD. AS THE DISTANCE FROM NORMANDY INCREASED THE SUPPLY PROBLEM BECAME ACUTE. STRONG ENEMY GARRISONS STILL HELD MOST OF THE CHANNEL PORTS, THUS PLACING A TREMENDOUS BURDEN UPON OUR LIMITED HARBOR FACILITIES. THE ACHIEVEMENT OF ARMY AND NAVY SUPPLY SERVICES IN SUSTAINING THE ADVANCING ARMIES CONTRIBUTED VITALLY TO THE LIBERATION OF NORTHERN FRANCE.

BY MID-SEPTEMBER, BRITISH AND CANADIAN TROOPS HAD FREED BRUSSELS AND ANTWERP AND ENTERED THE NETHERLANDS. THE U. S. FIRST ARMY HAD SWEPT ACROSS BELGIUM AND LUXEMBOURG TO THE GERMAN BORDER, WHILE THE THIRD ARMY, AIDED BY AIRBORNE SUPPLY, REACHED THE MOSELLE IN A RAPID ADVANCE. IN BRITTANY THE GARRISON OF BREST SURRENDERED TO THE NEWLY ACTIVATED NINTH ARMY ON 18 SEPTEMBER. ON THE RIGHT FLANK THE U. S. SEVENTH AND FRENCH FIRST ARMIES, SUPPORTED BY THE U. S. FIRST TACTICAL AIR FORCE, ADVANCED FROM THE BEACHES OF SOUTHERN FRANCE TO EXTEND THE ALLIED FRONT SOLIDLY TO THE SWISS FRONTIER.

PROGRESS IN THE NEXT THREE MONTHS WAS SLOW, THE FIGHTING BITTER, AS OPPOSITION STIFFENED. A MINOR AD-

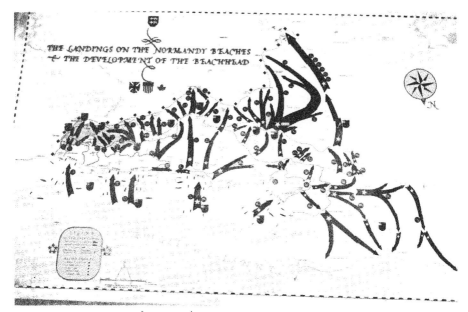

Beachhead Map—South Wall—South Loggia.

VANCE WAS EFFECTED IN THE NETHER-
LANDS WHEN THE ALLIED FIRST AIRBORNE
ARMY LANDED IN THE ARNHEM-EINDHOV-
EN AREA IN A VALIANT BUT UNSUCCESSFUL
EFFORT TO SEIZE THE CROSSINGS OF THE
LOWER RHINE; THERE FOLLOWED A
SERIES OF GALLANT AMPHIBIOUS OPERA-
ATIONS TO CLEAR THE WATER AP-
PROACHES TO THE PORT OF ANTWERP.
IN THE CENTER, AMERICAN TROOPS
BROKE THROUGH THE SIEGFRIED LINE,
SEIZED AACHEN, AND FOUGHT THEIR
WAY TO THE ROER RIVER. FARTHER
SOUTH THE FORTRESS OF METZ CAPITU-
LATED AFTER A BITTER STRUGGLE,
WHILE ON THE RIGHT FLANK THE
AMERICANS AND FRENCH REACHED THE
RHINE AT STRASBOURG AND MULHOUSE.

IN THE ARDENNES ON 16 DECEMBER
THE ENEMY LAUNCHED HIS FINAL MAJOR
COUNTER-OFFENSIVE, UNLEASHING THREE
ARMIES ON A NARROW FRONT. THE
STALWART DEFENSE AND SUPERB FIGHT-
ING SKILL OF THE AMERICAN SOLDIER
FINALLY HALTED THIS DRIVE. PROMPT
AND CONTINUOUS COUNTERMEASURES BY
GROUND AND AIR FORCES SUCCEEDED IN
ELIMINATING THE GERMAN SALIENT BY

MID-JANUARY. ON NEW YEAR'S EVE AN
ENEMY ATTACK NEAR COLMAR WAS ALSO
REPULSED AFTER A FURIOUS STRUGGLE.

ALLIED OPERATIONS TO CLEAR THE
WEST BANK OF THE RHINE IN FEBRUARY
AND EARLY MARCH WERE BRILLIANTLY
SUCCESSFUL; THE ARMIES INTENDED FOR
THE DEFENSE OF GERMANY WERE SHAT-
TERED BEYOND REPAIR. IN RAPID SUC-
CESSION, OUR FORCES THEN SEIZED A
BRIDGE AT REMAGEN, FORCED A CROSS-
ING AT OPPENHEIM, AND STAGED THEIR
MAJOR AMPHIBIOUS AND AIRBORNE AS-
SAULT NORTH OF THE RUHR VALLEY.
AS OUR GROUND FORCES RUSHED EAST-
WARD, PRECEDED BY AIRCRAFT WHICH
HARASSED AND DEMORALIZED THE RE-
TREATING ENEMY, THE RUHR WAS
ENCIRCLED IN A GIGANTIC DOUBLE
ENVELOPMENT. SWEEPING THROUGH
GERMANY THE ALLIED ARMIES MET THE
ADVANCING TROOPS OF THE U. S. S. R. AT
THE ELBE. HIS FORCES HAVING COM-
PLETELY DISINTEGRATED, THE ENEMY
CAPITULATED ON 8 MAY 1945, THUS
BRINGING TO AN END THE CAMPAIGN
BEGUN ELEVEN MONTHS BEFORE ON THE
BEACHES OF NORMANDY.

Overall Map—North Wall—North Loggia.

These maps were designed by Robert Foster of New York City from data furnished by the American Battle Monuments Commission. They were executed by Maurice Schmit of Paris. The panels in the ceilings of the loggias are of blue ceramic by Gentil & Bourdet of Paris.

The west face of the loggias bears the dedicatory inscription: "1941–1945 ☆ IN PROUD REMEMBRANCE OF THE ACHIEVEMENTS OF HER SONS AND IN HUMBLE TRIBUTE TO THEIR SACRIFICES THIS MEMORIAL HAS BEEN ERECTED BY THE UNITED STATES OF AMERICA", together with a French translation.

At the entrance to each loggia are two large bronze urns, also designed and sculptured in high relief by Donald De Lue and cast by Marinelli foundry of Florence, Italy. There are two identical pairs. On the face of one urn a dying warrior holding the sword with which he has fought the good fight is astride a charging horse which symbolizes War. The Angel of the Lord supports him and receives his spirit. On the reverse side of this urn a woman kneels, holding her child, beside the wreath-decorated grave of a soldier. About them shines the Star of Eternal Life. This composition is dedicated to the sacrifices and hardships of the women and children bereaved by war. The laurel leaf design around the top is symbolic of Victory and Honor.

On one side of the other urn, a figure represents the Lord as related in Genesis, Chapter I: "The spirit of the Lord moved on the face of the waters". The spray of laurel, on the representation of the waters, recalls to memory those who lost their lives at sea. The rainbow is the symbol of hope and peace. The reverse side of this urn shows a figure of an angel pushing away the stone—symbolic of resurrection and eternal life.

Standing on the platform and facing west, one sees in the foreground the reflecting pool; beyond it are the two flagstaffs, and the graves area with the chapel set at the intersection of the main avenues which are laid out as the arms of the Cross. To the north is the beach and English Channel. As late as 1956 it was still possible to see remnants of the so-called "Mulberry", the artificial port created by sinking ships and concrete caissons to facilitate the landing of our men and supplies. The Mulberry was installed a few days after the first assault, but was wrecked by a storm two weeks later. Nevertheless, hundreds of thousands of troops, and millions of tons of equipment and supplies were landed over this and neighboring beaches. Soon it became possible to draw gasoline through pipe-lines laid across the English Channel.

The memorial is built of Vaurion, a French limestone from the Cote d'Or region; the plinths and steps are of Ploumenach granite from Brittany. The pavement on the platform between the loggias is faced with pebbles taken from the invasion beach below the cliff.

THE GARDEN OF THE MISSING

On the east side of the memorial is the semicircular Garden of the Missing. Inscribed on its walls are the name, rank, organization and State of 1,557 of our Missing:

United States Army and Army
Air Forces [1] 1, 185
United States Navy......... 371
United States Coast Guard... 1

These gave their lives in the service of their country but their remains have not been identified, or they were buried at sea in this region. These men came from every State in the Union, as well as from the District of Columbia, Hawaii, and Guam.

The following inscriptions, with French translation, appear above these names:

"HERE ARE RECORDED THE NAMES OF AMERICANS WHO GAVE THEIR LIVES IN THE SERVICE OF THEIR COUNTRY AND WHO SLEEP IN UNKNOWN GRAVES".

"THIS IS THEIR MEMORIAL THE WHOLE EARTH THEIR SEPULCHRE".

"COMRADES IN ARMS WHOSE RESTING PLACE IS KNOWN ONLY TO GOD".

At the center of the west side of the garden and below the colonnade is inscribed this extract from the dedication by General Eisenhower of the "Golden Book" now enshrined in St. Paul's Cathedral, London:

"TO THESE WE OWE THE HIGH RESOLVE THAT THE CAUSE FOR WHICH THEY DIED SHALL LIVE".

The garden has beds of Polyantha roses "Joseph Guy"; European Ash trees (Fraxinus excelsior) grow in the lawn areas; the beds at the foot of the walls of the Missing are planted with heather (Erica coccinea) and boxwood (Boxus sempervirens).

THE GRAVES AREA

The 9,386 headstones are set in 10 plots. Their precise alignment upon the smooth green lawn conveys an unforgettable impression of dignity and beauty.

These Dead, who gave their lives in our Country's service, came from every State in the Union, the District of Columbia, Alaska, and Hawaii. A few of them came from England, Scotland, and Canada.

307 of the headstones mark the graves of "Unknowns".

Here, buried side by side, are a father and his son; here, also, in 30 instances two brothers rest side by side.

Informal groups of Japanese Rose and Sea Buckthorn are planted in the grave plots.

[1] It will be recalled that during World War II the Air Forces still formed part of the United States Army.

Memorial Urns.

The Garden of the Missing (South Wall).

The Chapel

EXTERIOR

The circular chapel, also built of Vaurion stone on Ploumenach granite steps, is surmounted by a bronze finial with an armillary sphere. To the south side of the entrance door are the inscriptions:

"THIS CHAPEL HAS BEEN ERECTED BY THE UNITED STATES OF AMERICA IN GRATEFUL MEMORY OF HER SONS WHO GAVE THEIR LIVES IN THE LANDINGS ON THE NORMANDY BEACHES AND IN THE LIBERATION OF NORTHERN FRANCE"

"THEIR GRAVES ARE THE PERMANENT AND VISIBLE SYMBOL OF THEIR HEROIC

11

DEVOTION AND THEIR SACRIFICE IN THE COMMON CAUSE OF HUMANITY".

A French translation of these texts is inscribed on the north side of the door. Around the frieze of the chapel is inscribed:

"THESE ENDURED ALL AND GAVE ALL THAT JUSTICE AMONG NATIONS MIGHT PREVAIL AND THAT MANKIND MIGHT ENJOY FREEDOM AND INHERIT PEACE".

In the frieze, and vertically above the door, is a replica of the Congressional Medal of Honor, our Country's highest and rarest award for valor beyond the call of duty.

INTERIOR

The chapel altar is of Pyrenees black and gold "Grand Antique" marble. It bears the inscription:

"I GIVE UNTO THEM ETERNAL LIFE AND THEY SHALL NEVER PERISH".

Above it a cross is silhouetted against the crystal window. The altar is flanked by the flags of the United States, France, Great Britain, and Canada. On the south wall (of French travertine limestone) is inscribed:

"THROUGH THE GATE OF DEATH MAY THEY PASS TO THEIR JOYFUL RESURRECTION".

This inscription is surmounted by a cross. Symmetrically opposite it, on the north side, is this inscription, surmounted by the Star of David and the Tablets of Moses:

"THINK NOT ONLY UPON THEIR PASSING REMEMBER THE GLORY OF THEIR SPIRIT".

CEILING

The mosaic ceiling, designed and executed by Leon Kroll of New York City, symbolizes America who gives her farewell blessing to her sons as they depart by sea and air to fight for her principles of freedom. Over the altar, a grateful France bestows a laurel wreath upon our Dead who gave their lives to liberate Europe's oppressed peoples. The return of Peace is recalled by the angel, the dove, and the homeward-bound ship.

MALL FEATURE

At the western end of the main axis of the cemetery are two Italian granite (Baveno) figures by Donald De Lue representing the United States and France.

THE CLIFF AREA

A low wall forms a parapet at the edge of the cliff overlooking Omaha Beach which may be reached by steps descending from the overlook at the eastern end of this wall. Prior to the 1944 landings the enemy had installed artillery and machine-guns along these cliffs so that he could fire lengthwise along the beaches; two casemates are visible just east of the cemetery boundary. From the beach one may gain some idea of the perils of those who on that June morning stormed ashore. Notwithstanding underwater obstacles and mines and this cross-enfilading fire, they strode forward to seize the cliffs and gain the first foothold in the liberation of France.

An orientation table at the overlook indicates the various landing beaches; along the path to the beach another orientation table shows the Mulberry in some detail.

The cemetery is surrounded on three sides by heavy masses of Austrian Pine (Pinus nigra), interplanted with Whitebeam (Sorbus aria), Russian Olive (Eleagnus angustifolia), Sea Buckthorn (Hippophae rhamnoides), Japanese Rose (Rosa rugosa), and French Tamarisk (Tamarix gallica). There is an avenue of Austrian Pine along the escarpment wall.

Formality is given to the planting at the Memorial with hedges of English Holly (Ilex aquifolium).

Construction of the cemetery and memorial was completed in 1956.

Youth Triumphing Over Evil—Brittany Memorial.
(Lee Lawrie, Sculptor.)

AMERICAN MILITARY
𝔊emeteries & 𝔐emorials
OF WORLD WAR II

THE AMERICAN BATTLE MONUMENTS COMMISSION is responsible to the people of the United States for the construction and permanent maintenance of military cemeteries and memorials built by the United States Government on foreign soil. It is not responsible for construction, maintenance, or operation of cemeteries in the continental United States or its Territories and possessions.

After World War I the American Battle Monuments Commission erected a memorial chapel in each of the eight

To the Missing—World War II Loggia—Suresnes. (*Lewis Iselin, Sculptor.*)

military cemeteries already established by the War Department, as well as eleven monuments and two bronze tablets on the battlefields and elsewhere, to record the achievements of our Armed Forces.[1]

By the end of World War II several hundred temporary cemeteries had been established by the American Graves Registration Service of the United States Army. During the years 1947 to 1954 that Service, complying with the expressed wishes of the next-of-kin, and by authority of law, repatriated the remains of some 171,000, representing 61 per cent of the recovered bodies. The remaining 39 per cent were given final interment in the cemeteries on foreign soil; and in the

cemeteries at Honolulu, Sitka and Puerto Rico (which remain under Army control).

Fourteen sites in foreign countries were selected as permanent cemeteries in 1947 by the Secretary of the Army, with the assistance of the American Battle Monuments Commission. Their locations reflect the progress of the

---

[1] These were: Cemeteries: Brookwood, England; Suresnes, Oise-Aisne (Fere-en-Tardenois), Aisne-Marne (B e l l e a u), Somme (Bony), St. Mihiel (Thiaucourt), Meuse-Argonne (R o m a g n e), France; Waregem, Belgium. Monuments: Brest, Cantigny, Bellicourt, Chateau-Thierry, Somme-Py, Montfaucon, Montsec, Tours, France; Kemmel, Audenarde, Belgium; Gibraltar. Tablets: Chaumont, Souilly, France.

military operations; they were selected with a view to their accessibility, aspeet, prospect, drainage, and other practical considerations. In every case use of the site in perpetuity was granted by the host government to the United States, free of cost, rent, and taxes. The remainder of the "temporary" cemetery sites reverted to the landowners upon completion of reburial operations.

The fourteen permanent World War II cemeteries with numbers of graves including Unknowns, and the numbers of Missing recorded at the Memorials are:

	Dead	Unknown	List of Missing
Cambridge, England............	3,811 including.....	24	5, 125
Normandy (near St. Laurent sur Mer, Calvados), France.	9,386 including.....	307	1, 557
Brittany (near St. James, Manche), France.	4,410 including.....	95	498
Epinal, France.................	5,255 including.....	69	424
Lorraine (at St. Avold, Moselle), France.	10,489 including....	151	444
Rhône (at Draguignan, Var), France.	861 including......	62	293
Netherlands (near Margraten), Holland.	8,301 including.....	105	1, 722
Henri-Chapelle, Belgium.........	7,989 including.....	89	451
Ardennes (near Neuville-en-Condroz), Belgium.	5,244 including.....	744	465
Luxembourg (at Hamm, near Luxembourg), Luxembourg.	5,076 including.....	101	372
Florence, Italy.................	4,402 including.....	212	1, 409
Sicily-Rome (Nettuno, near Rome), Italy.	7,860 including.....	488	3, 095
North Africa (near Carthage), Tunisia.	2,840 including.....	240	3, 725
Philippines (near Manila)........	17,178 including....	3, 744	36, 269

In addition, 24 Unknowns of World War II were interred in the World War I cemetery at Suresnes, near Paris.[2]

The following World War II cemeteries are maintained by the Department of the Army:

	Dead	Unknown	List of Missing
Honolulu, T. H.[3]...............	13,510 including ...	2, 009	18, 106
Puerto Rico....................	69................	......	......
Sitka, Alaska..................	72 including.......	5	

In 1947 the American Battle Monuments Commission selected fourteen outstanding American architects, each to design one of the cemeteries, conceiving the graves plots and a monument as complementary elements of an

[2] See page 18 concerning World War II memorial.
[3] See page 21 concerning memorial.

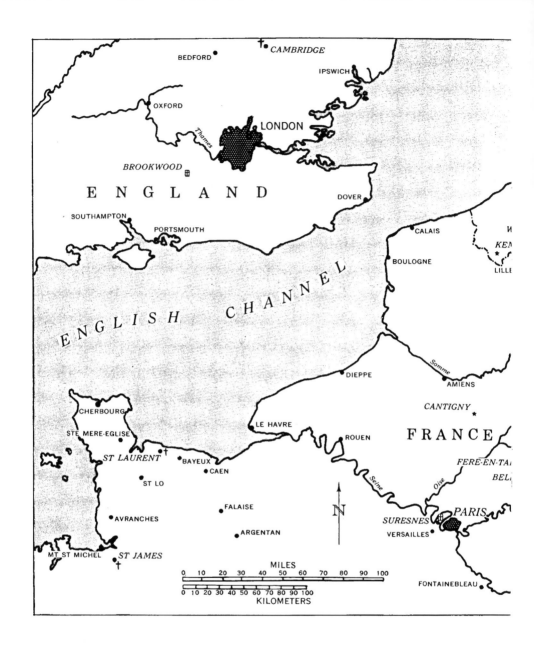

integral memorial to the services and sacrifices of the American Armed Services who fought in the respective regions. Upon approval of the general schemes by the Commission, and by agreement with the Secretary of the Army, the architects' plans of the graves plots were followed by the American Graves Registration Service in making the permanent burials of those remains which, by decision of the next-of-kin, were to remain overseas. This timely cooperation of the two agencies contributed appreciably to the coherence of the development of the cemetery designs.

Beginning in the latter half of 1949, the permanent interments having been

virtually completed, the cemeteries were progressively transferred to the American Battle Monuments Commission by Executive Order, for construction and maintenance. Thereupon the remaining portions of the architects' designs were carried out, step by step—grading; installation of a system of reinforced-concrete beams on piles to maintain the levels and alignments of the headstones; fabrication and installation of the headstones; construction of water-supply and distribution systems; utilities buildings; roads and paths; plantings; and the erection of the memorials.

To provide against dry seasons and the occasional real drought, each cemetery is equipped with storage reservoirs and a high-pressure sprinkling system.

For the design of the various memorials no specific requirement was imposed upon the architects beyond the budgeted cost, except that each should embody these features:

A small devotional chapel.
Inscription of the names and particulars of the Missing in the region.
A graphic record, in permanent form, of the services of our troops.

These requirements have been interpreted in a wide, and interesting, variety of forms.

An important motive for the construction of the memorials was the implied undertaking by our Government to record by monuments the achievements of our Armed Services, since, by Department orders, the erection of monuments by the troops (which unfortunately have been found to be often poorly-designed, poorly constructed and lacking provision for maintenance) was expressly forbidden. The "permanent graphic" record takes the form of maps, usually quite large murals, amplified by descriptive texts in English as well as the language of the country in which the cemetery is situated. The historical data (in the form of map layouts and texts) were prepared by the American Battle Monuments Commission; the maps were rendered in tasteful presentation by experienced artists. In no two cases is the method—or even the materials—the same; the map may be of layered marbles, or in fresco, perhaps in bronze relief, or in ceramics. Another feature of interest at each memorial is the two sets of "Key-Maps": "The War Against Germany" and "The War Against Japan". Each set consists of three maps, each covering about one-third of the period of our participation in the war. By these Key-Maps each major battle may be related to all others in time and space.

With each architect an American landscape architect, an American sculptor and an American muralist or painter ordinarily collaborated. Their talents have made a major contribution to the beauty and dignity of the Memorials all of which are dedicated to the memory of the achievements of those who served and of the sacrifices of those who died. The construction of the cemeteries and memorials, as well as of most of the works of art, was effected by local contractors and artists under the supervision of the Commission.

Each grave is marked by a headstone of white marble, of the same designs as those used in the overseas cemeteries of World War I—a Star of David for those of Jewish faith, a Latin Cross for all others. These headstones were quarried and fabricated in the Italian Tyrol, northwest of Venice, except about one-half of those at the Philippines cemetery which came from the region of Carrara in western Italy. Each headstone bears the deceased's name, rank, service number, organization, date of death, and State or Territory from which he entered the military service. Headstones of the Unknowns, i. e., those remains which could not be identified, bear the inscription: HERE RESTS IN HONORED GLORY A COMRADE IN ARMS KNOWN BUT TO GOD.

The lists of Missing (which include the unidentified and those lost and buried at sea) give name, rank, organization and State; the conditions under which death occurred were usually such as to deny the possibility of recording the exact date.

In addition to the fourteen World War II cemeteries and Memorials, the American Battle Monuments Commission program includes the following:

SURESNES

As previously stated, 24 World War II Unknowns were interred in this World War I cemetery. Here, where senior representatives of the French and United States Governments on ceremonial occasions pay homage to our Dead, the World War I chapel was, by addition of two loggias, converted

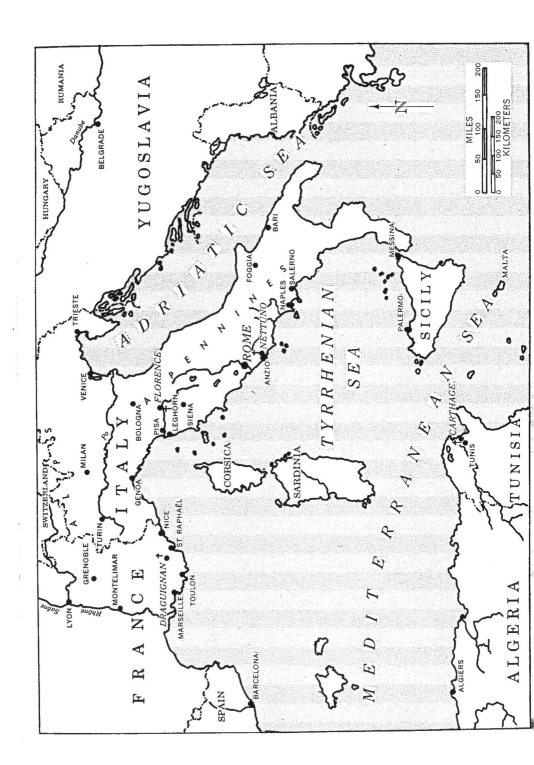

"Memory"—World War II Memorial Chamber—Suresnes. (*Lewis Iselin, Sculptor.*)

into a shrine to commemorate our Dead of both wars.

The wall of the World War II loggia bears this inscription:

TO THE ETERNAL MEMORY OF 358,967 AMERICANS WHO GAVE THEIR LIVES IN THE SERVICE OF THEIR COUNTRY DURING WORLD WAR II. OF THIS HOST 106,757 REST IN EIGHTEEN OVERSEAS MILITARY CEMETERIES. THE REMAINS OF 174,426 WERE RETURNED TO THEIR HOMELAND. OF THOSE RESTING IN THE OVERSEAS MILITARY CEMETERIES 8,494 HAVE NOT BEEN IDENTIFIED. THEIRS ARE AMONG THE 78,966 NAMES OF THOSE MISSING IN ACTION OR LOST OR BURIED AT SEA WHICH ARE RECORDED UPON THE WALLS OF THE CEMETERY MEMORIALS. * * * INTO THY HANDS O LORD.

Within the World War II memorial chamber is engraved:

THIS MEMORIAL HAS BEEN ERECTED BY THE UNITED STATES OF AMERICA IN PROUD AND GRATEFUL MEMORY OF HER SOLDIERS, SAILORS, MARINES AND AIRMEN WHO LAID DOWN THEIR LIVES IN ALL QUARTERS OF THE EARTH THAT OTHER PEOPLES MIGHT BE FREED FROM OPPRESSION * * * LET US HERE HIGHLY RESOLVE THAT THESE HONORED DEAD SHALL NOT HAVE DIED IN VAIN.

EAST COAST MEMORIAL

To commemorate those 4,596 Americans who, in or above the waters off the east coasts of North and South America, gave their lives in the service of their Country their names, and particulars are to be inscribed on a memorial to be erected at New York.

WEST COAST MEMORIAL

Similarly, the names and particulars of those 412 Americans who gave their lives in the service of their Country off the west coasts of the Americas will be recorded at a memorial to be erected at San Francisco.

HONOLULU MEMORIAL

Although the military cemetery at Honolulu is maintained by the Department of the Army, the American Battle Monuments Commission, by agreement with the Secretary of the Army, will erect a memorial therein, similar in objects to those built in the other overseas cemeteries. Buried at the cemetery are 13,510 Dead of World War II and 1,200 who died in the Korean operations; the Memorial will record 18,106 Missing of World War II and 8,000 Missing in Korea. The memorial will also embody the customary chapel and maps.

MAINTENANCE

Permanent maintenance of the cemeteries is a responsibility of the American Battle Monuments Commission. The Superintendent and Assistant Superintendent in each case are American war veterans.

At each cemetery there is a Visitors' Building, with comfortably furnished reception room. Here visitors may be informed as to the location of graves (or inscription of the Missing) at any overseas cemetery.

The cemeteries are open every day of the year. Photography is permitted at the cemeteries and monuments without special authorization, except when photography is to be used for commercial purposes—in such case permission must be obtained from the Commission's local office.

Unlike the national cemeteries under the jurisdiction of the Quartermaster General, Department of the Army, there can be no further burials in the American military cemeteries overseas except of those remains which may, in the future, be found on the battlefields.

FLOWERS

In the general interest, the decoration of graves with natural cut flowers only is permitted. The Commission is happy to assist interested persons to arrange with local florists in foreign countries for placing such decorations. Requests should be mailed so as to arrive at the appropriate Commission office at least 5 days before the date of decoration and should be accompanied by check or international money order in dollars or local currency. Deposits may be made for a single decoration on a particular day—birthday, Memorial Day, Christmas Day, for example—or for several decorations on particular dates within the year or over a period of years. Checks should be made payable to "The American Battle Monuments Commission, Flower Fund", money orders to "The American Battle Monuments Commission". Requests should be addressed to the Commission's Paris office, except in the case of Florence, Sicily-Rome (Nettuno) and North Africa (Carthage) Cemeteries where the Rome office is responsible, and Manila where the Manila office is responsible.

Orders for flowers for all cemeteries may also be placed through any local florist who is a member of the "Florists Telegraph Delivery Association." In addition to the name of the deceased, the rank, service number, name of the cemetery, country in which located, and the location by plot, row, and grave should be provided if known.

Further information regarding cemeteries and memorials may be obtained at the Commission's offices in Washington, Paris, Rome, or Manila. Visitors passing through these cities are invited to call. The Commission's representatives there may be of some assistance in verifying travel routes and schedules, and also in furnishing information concerning overnight accommodations.

PHOTOGRAPHS

Upon the request of the bona fide next of kin, the Commission will furnish one photograph of the appropriate headstone or inscription engraved on the Wall of the Missing.

Suresnes Memorial With World War I and II Loggias.

THE AMERICAN BATTLE MONUMENTS COMMISSION

United States Office

Washington 25, D. C.
Telephone: Liberty 5–6700
      Extension 63679
Telegrams: Monuments, Washington

Mediterranean Office

American Embassy,
Via Veneto, Rome
Telephone: 414, Extension 156
Telegrams: Monuments, Rome

European Office

20 rue Quentin Bauchart
Paris, 8e, France
Telephone: Balzac 0700
Telegrams: Monuments, Paris

Philippine Office

American Military Cemetery,
Manila, P. I.
Telephone: 5–02–12
Telegrams: AMBAMCOM, Manila,
    P. I.

THE AMERICAN BATTLE MONUMENTS COMMISSION
Established by Congress March 1923

Membership (December 1956)

George C. Marshall, *Chairman*
Thomas C. Kinkaid, *Vice Chairman*
Leslie L. Biffle
Alexander A. Vandegrift
Charles E. Potter
John Phillips

Mrs. Theodore Roosevelt
Mrs. Wendell L. Willkie
Carl Spaatz
Benjamin O. Davis
Forest A. Harness
Thomas North, *Secretary*

Former Members

John J. Pershing	1923–48	Mrs. Henry Fenimore Baker	1930–53
Robert G. Woodside	1923–53	Burnet R. Maybank	1946–53
David A. Reed	1923–47	Joseph C. Baldwin	1946–53
J. P. B. Clayton Hill	1923–41	Edward C. Kalbfus	1947–53
Thomas W. Miller	1923–26	Harold A. Keats	1950–53
Mrs. Frederic W. Bentley	1923–29	Joseph J. Foss	1953–55
D. John Markey	1923–53	X. H. Price, *Secretary*	1923–38
Finis J. Garrett	1926–53		

Consulting Architects

Paul P. Cret (World War I program)
Harbeson, Hough, Livingston & Larson (World War II program)

Consulting Landscape Architect

Markley Stevenson (World War II program)

Consulting Sculptor

Lee Lawrie (World War II program)